Chapter Lis

2-3-5 Est 1890's

"WM" 3-2-2-3 Est Mid 1920's

"Total Football" Est 1970's

4-4-2 Est 1960's

Tiki Taka 4-3-3 Est 2006

Inverted FullBack/Hybrid Systems Est 2010's

Introduction:

Football, the beautiful game, has evolved dramatically over the years. It's not just about kicking a ball into the net; it's about strategy, tactics, and formations that have shaped the way the sport is played. From the rudimentary formations of the early 19th century to the intricate tactical systems of the modern era, the development of football formations tells a compelling story of innovation, adaptation, and the pursuit of excellence on the pitch.

This book delves deep into the history of football tactics, providing an in-depth analysis of how formations have evolved to meet the ever-changing demands of the game. This book takes you on a journey through time, exploring the key moments and figures who have influenced the way football is played, from the chaotic early days to the era of data-driven analysis and artificial intelligence.

In the following chapters, we will examine the pivotal moments in the evolution of football formations. We'll revisit the days when football was still finding its identity and formations resembled more of a chaotic scramble for the ball than a structured game plan. We'll witness the rise of classic formations like the 2-3-5 Pyramid and the W-M formation, which laid the groundwork for tactical innovation.

This book will then take you through the eras of Total Football, Catenaccio, and the 4-4-2 formation, showcasing how different countries and managers approached the game. You'll learn about the iconic teams and players who left their mark on football history.

As we progress through the chapters, we'll explore the tactical revolutions brought about by visionary coaches like Rinus Michels, Pep Guardiola, and Jurgen Klopp. We'll also discuss the impact of technological advancements on the game, such as video analysis and artificial intelligence, and how they have transformed coaching and strategy.

This is not just a history book; it's a strategic analysis of how football has adapted and continues to adapt to the challenges of the modern world. Whether you're a die-hard football fan, a coach, or simply someone fascinated by the tactical intricacies of the sport, this book will provide you with a comprehensive understanding of how football formations have shaped the game we know and love today.

So, join us on this journey through time and tactics as we explore the fascinating and ever-changing world of football formations, from the birth of the sport to the cutting-edge strategies of the 21st century. Let's kick off the adventure by delving into the early days of football in Chapter 1: "The Birth of Football: Formation Anarchy."

Chapter 1: The Birth of Football - Formation Anarchy

In the dimly lit, muddy fields of 19th-century England, the game of football was a far cry from the sleek, organized sport we know today. It was a chaotic, almost lawless endeavor, with little semblance of formation or tactics. This chapter transports us back to the origins of football, a time when players gathered to kick a ball around with minimal rules and structure.

The Primordial Chaos

Picture this: a vast, open field with no boundary lines, no goalposts, and no standardized ball. Teams were often arbitrary, determined by the number of players available, and the goal was simple - get the ball to the opposing team's end. The concept of positions and formations was virtually nonexistent. Matches were raucous affairs, resembling more of a brawl than a sport. The ball was often a pig's bladder, and the rules governing its use were ambiguous at best. Players were unrestrained, and the absence of referees meant that any form of foul play was met with fists rather than whistles.

Early Signs of Structure

As football began to grow in popularity, players and spectators alike recognized the need for some semblance of order. This was the embryonic stage of football formations. While not as structured as we understand them today, rudimentary patterns began to emerge.

Players started to gravitate towards specific roles based on their skills. Those who were faster and more agile naturally found themselves chasing the ball, while stronger individuals positioned themselves closer to the goal, both as protectors and potential scorers. This rudimentary division of labor started to lay the foundation for what would later become recognizable positions.

The Birth of the 2-3-5 Formation

In the midst of this anarchy, a glimmer of tactical thinking emerged. The 2-3-5 formation, often referred to as the "pyramid," took shape. It was a formation with two defenders, three midfielders, and five forwards.

While far from the meticulously planned tactics of modern football, this represented a fundamental shift towards organization. The 2-3-5 formation, with its staggered arrangement of players, allowed for a more methodical approach to attack and defense. It provided a basic structure for players to understand their roles on the pitch. Yet, it was still a far cry from the tactical sophistication we see today.

The Legacy of Formation Anarchy

Chapter 1 explores the groundwork for understanding how football evolved from a free-for-all on the field to a meticulously orchestrated game with complex tactical systems.As we move forward in this journey through football's tactical history, we'll witness the revolutionary moments and visionary thinkers who transformed the game from this anarchic state to the highly structured and strategic sport we know today. Join us in Chapter 2 as we delve into "The 2-3-5 Pyramid: Early Dominance" and discover how this formation set the stage for the tactical innovations that would follow.

Chapter 2: The 2-3-5 Pyramid: Early Dominance

In the early days of organized football, the 2-3-5 formation, often referred to as the "pyramid," reigned supreme. This chapter delves into an era when this formation dominated the football landscape and how it shaped the sport's tactics and strategies.

The Pyramid Takes Center Stage

As the 19th century transitioned into the 20th, the 2-3-5 formation emerged as the prevailing tactical system. This formation consisted of two defenders, three midfielders, and five forwards. While it may seem incredibly front-heavy by today's standards, it was a formation that perfectly suited the football of its time.

The two defenders provided a semblance of defense, the three midfielders acted as a link between defense and attack, and the five forwards were tasked with both scoring goals and putting immense pressure on the opposing defense. This formation favored attacking play, often resulting in high-scoring matches.

Key Features of the Pyramid

The 2-3-5 formation was characterized by its simplicity and aggression. Full-backs, as they would be known today, were still in their infancy, and the concept of a defensive midfielder had not yet taken root. The formation thrived on the principles of fluidity and improvisation.

Players in the pyramid formation had to be versatile. A forward could suddenly find themselves defending, and vice versa. The lack of defined positions meant that footballers needed to possess a wide range of skills, from dribbling to tackling and goal-scoring.

The Great Forwards of the Pyramid Era

One of the most iconic aspects of the 2-3-5 formation was the prominence of legendary forwards who graced the football fields of the time. Players like Dixie Dean, George Camsell, and Jimmy McGrory became household names, their goal-scoring exploits celebrated across the footballing world.

These forwards were not constrained by the modern-day distinctions between strikers, wingers, or attacking midfielders. Instead, they roamed freely, combining teamwork with individual brilliance to create goal-scoring opportunities. The 2-3-5 formation allowed these players to shine and become legends of the game.

The Decline of the Pyramid

While the 2-3-5 formation was incredibly successful during its heyday, it eventually began to show its limitations. Opponents adapted their tactics, focusing on exploiting the space left by the lack of defensive cover in the midfield. This led to a decline in the formation's effectiveness.

Additionally, rule changes, such as the offside law modifications in 1925, forced teams to reconsider their tactical approach. As the game continued to evolve, the need for more structured and defensively sound formations became evident.

Legacy of the Pyramid

The 2-3-5 formation left an indelible mark on the history of football. It was the first step in the evolution of football tactics, paving the way for more complex and versatile formations. The pyramid era showcased the importance of fluidity, teamwork, and adaptability on the pitch.

As we progress through this exploration of football formation evolution, we'll witness how the 2-3-5 pyramid laid the foundation for future innovations. The sport was rapidly evolving, and tactical minds were eager to experiment and refine their approaches.

Join us in Chapter 3 as we delve into "The WM Formation: Herbert Chapman's Revolution" and discover how this formation signaled the next phase in football's tactical development, bringing with it new challenges and opportunities for coaches and players alike.

Chapter 3: The W-M Formation: Herbert Chapman's Revolution

The transition from the 2-3-5 pyramid to the W-M formation marked a significant turning point in the history of football tactics. In this chapter, we explore how Herbert Chapman's innovative approach reshaped the game and introduced a more structured and adaptable formation.

The Genesis of the W-M Formation

Herbert Chapman, the visionary manager of Huddersfield Town and later Arsenal, is credited with popularizing the W-M formation in the 1920s. This formation, which resembled the letters 'W' and 'M' when viewed from above, represented a fundamental shift in tactical thinking.

The W-M formation featured three defenders, two defensive midfielders, two inside forwards, and three forwards. It was a departure from the heavily front-loaded 2-3-5 pyramid and introduced a more balanced and organized approach to the game.

The Defensive Innovation

One of the most significant contributions of the W-M formation was its emphasis on defensive solidity. Chapman recognized the need for a formation that could defend effectively without compromising attacking options. By employing two defensive midfielders, he created a protective shield in front of the defense, preventing opponents from easily penetrating the center of the pitch.

This newfound defensive resilience was crucial in an era when football was becoming more competitive, and teams were becoming more tactically astute. Chapman's Arsenal became known for their disciplined defense, a hallmark of the W-M formation.

Fluidity and Adaptability

While the 2-3-5 had limited positional roles, the W-M formation introduced greater structure. Inside forwards and center-forwards had distinct roles, and players were expected to stick to their positions more diligently. This allowed for better coordination and a more versatile approach to attack.

The Defensive Innovation

One of the most significant contributions of the W-M formation was its emphasis on defensive solidity. Chapman recognized the need for a formation that could defend effectively without compromising attacking options. By employing two defensive midfielders, he created a protective shield in front of the defense, preventing opponents from easily penetrating the center of the pitch.

This newfound defensive resilience was crucial in an era when football was becoming more competitive, and teams were becoming more tactically astute. Chapman's Arsenal became known for their disciplined defense, a hallmark of the W-M formation.

Fluidity and Adaptability

While the 2-3-5 had limited positional roles, the W-M formation introduced greater structure. Inside forwards and center-forwards had distinct roles, and players were expected to stick to their positions more diligently. This allowed for better coordination and a more versatile approach to attack.

Chapman's Legacy

Herbert Chapman's tactical innovations extended beyond the W-M formation. He was one of the first managers to use floodlights for evening matches, implement a shirt numbering system, and introduce warm-up routines for players. His forward-thinking approach to the game set the standard for modern football management.

Chapman's influence extended to future generations of managers, who drew inspiration from his methods. The W-M formation, although eventually replaced by newer tactical systems, had a lasting impact on football's tactical evolution.

The W-M Formation in Modern Football

While the W-M formation is no longer the dominant tactical system in modern football, its principles of defensive organization, adaptability, and specialization continue to influence the sport. Managers today often draw upon these foundational ideas when developing their strategies.

In the chapters to come, we will explore further innovations in football formations and tactics, including the advent of Total Football, the rise of Italian Catenaccio, and the global impact of the 4-4-2 formation. Join us in Chapter 4 as we dive into "Total Football: Rinus Michels and the Dutch Innovation," where we'll discover how a small nation revolutionized the beautiful game with their inventive approach to football.

Chapter 4: Total Football: Rinus Michels and the Dutch Innovation

In the annals of football history, few tactical revolutions have been as transformative as Total Football, a revolutionary approach that originated in the Netherlands under the guidance of Rinus Michels. Chapter 4 delves into the inception and impact of Total Football, a system that forever changed the way the game was played.

The Birth of Total Football

Total Football, or "Totaalvoetbal" in Dutch, was a tactical philosophy that emphasized fluidity, positional interchangeability, and high pressing. It was a radical departure from the traditional static positions of players, and it sought to create a dynamic, harmonious system where players seamlessly switched roles during the course of a match.

Rinus Michels, the pioneering manager, first introduced this concept in the 1960s while coaching Ajax Amsterdam. The system relied on players who were not only technically proficient but also possessed a deep understanding of the game, capable of adapting to various positions and roles as the need arose.

Key Principles of Total Football

Total Football was built on several fundamental principles:

- Positional Fluidity: Players were not restricted to fixed positions; they were encouraged to rotate, interchange, and cover for each other, ensuring constant movement and unpredictability.

- High Pressing: Total Football teams pressed high up the pitch, aiming to win the ball back quickly and disrupt the opponent's build-up play.

- Compactness: When defending, the team maintained a compact shape, minimizing space for the opposition to exploit.

- Technical Proficiency: Players were required to be adept at passing, dribbling, and decision-making, as these skills were crucial to the system's success.

The Ajax and Netherlands Era

Under Rinus Michels' guidance, Ajax Amsterdam and later the Dutch national team became synonymous with Total Football. Ajax achieved unprecedented success, winning three consecutive European Cups from 1971 to 1973. This success was mirrored on the international stage, as the Netherlands reached the 1974 World Cup final playing an exhilarating brand of Total Football.

Key figures like Johan Cruyff, Johan Neeskens, and Ruud Krol embodied the Total Football philosophy. Cruyff, in particular, became the system's poster child, showcasing the brilliance of positional interchangeability and individual skill.

Total Football's Global Impact

The impact of Total Football extended far beyond the Netherlands. Coaches around the world took notice of its effectiveness and sought to incorporate elements of the system into their own teams. The tactical landscape of football was forever changed as the principles of Total Football spread.

lTotal Football's Modern Legacy

While Total Football as practiced in its purest form may be rare today, its principles continue to influence modern football. High pressing, fluidity in attack, and the importance of versatile players are all hallmarks of this revolutionary system.

n the chapters ahead, we will continue our journey through the evolution of football formations, examining the defensive resilience of Catenaccio, the rise of the 4-4-2 formation, and the artistic mastery of Spain's Tiki-Taka. Join us in Chapter 5, where we explore "The Rise of Catenaccio: Italy's Defensive Prowess," and discover how Italy's tactical innovation became a formidable force in the world of football.

Chapter 5: The Rise of Catenaccio: Italy's Defensive Prowess

In the fascinating tapestry of football tactics, the emergence of Catenaccio stands as a testament to Italy's mastery of defensive strategy. Chapter 5 transports us to an era when Italian teams became synonymous with defensive resilience, showcasing how Catenaccio rose to prominence.

The Birth of Catenaccio

Catenaccio, an Italian term meaning "door bolt" or "safety lock," was a tactical system that prioritized defensive solidity and organization. It was a direct response to the attacking philosophies of Total Football and other free-flowing systems that had gained popularity in the 1960s.

The key feature of Catenaccio was the implementation of a sweeper, or "libero," positioned behind the defensive line. This sweeper acted as a safety net, ready to sweep up any threats posed by the opponent's forwards. The rest of the team, including full-backs and midfielders, operated with a strong emphasis on defending, often forming a deep, compact defensive block.

The Defensive Structure

Catenaccio relied on a structured, disciplined defense that aimed to deny the opponent space and opportunities. Defenders were expected to maintain their positions rigorously, closing down attackers, and minimizing risks. The compactness of the defensive block made it challenging for opponents to penetrate.

The sweeper, a pivotal figure in Catenaccio, would aggressively intercept through balls and launch counterattacks when the opportunity arose. This role demanded exceptional reading of the game and ball-playing skills.

Catenaccio's Success

Catenaccio was highly successful in Italy and beyond during the 1960s and 1970s. Inter Milan, under the management of Helenio Herrera, became the embodiment of Catenaccio's defensive excellence. The team won multiple Serie A titles and the European Cup, showcasing the effectiveness of this tactical approach.

Italian national teams also adopted Catenaccio principles, leading to international success. The Azzurri won the 1982 FIFA World Cup with a disciplined, defensively astute approach that bore the hallmarks of Catenaccio.

Criticism and Evolution

While Catenaccio achieved great success, it also faced criticism for its perceived negativity. Detractors argued that it stifled creativity and led to overly defensive football. However, proponents of Catenaccio emphasized its tactical sophistication and the art of defending.

Over time, Catenaccio evolved as coaches sought to find a balance between defensive solidity and attacking flair. The sweeper position gradually faded, and Italian teams adopted more modern formations while preserving the defensive discipline instilled by Catenaccio

Catenaccio's Legacy

Catenaccio's legacy endures in the DNA of Italian football. The emphasis on defense, tactical intelligence, and disciplined organization remains a hallmark of Italian teams. Even in the modern era, Italy has continued to produce world-class defenders and maintain a strong defensive identity.

In the upcoming chapters, we will explore the tactical evolution of football further, delving into the global impact of the 4-4-2 formation, the rise of Spain's Tiki-Taka, and the versatility of the 4-3-3 formation. Join us in Chapter 6, where we uncover "The 4-4-2 Era: England's World Cup Triumph," and discover how this formation became a symbol of English football during a historic period.

Chapter 6: The 4-4-2 Era: England's World Cup Triumph

The 4-4-2 formation, often hailed as a classic and straightforward system, played a pivotal role in shaping the identity of English football. Chapter 6 takes us back to a time when this formation reigned supreme, culminating in England's historic World Cup victory.

The Emergence of the 4-4-2 Formation

The 4-4-2 formation, characterized by four defenders, four midfielders, and two strikers, provided a balanced and pragmatic approach to the game. While it may appear conventional, its simplicity and versatility made it highly effective.

In this formation, the midfield was typically split into two central midfielders and two wide midfielders, creating a solid core while allowing for width in attack. The two strikers operated as a pair, often with one serving as the target man and the other as the poacher.

The Triumph of England in 1966

The golden moment for the 4-4-2 formation came in 1966 when England hosted and won the FIFA World Cup. Managed by Sir Alf Ramsey, the England team used the 4-4-2 system as the backbone of their success.

The 4-4-2 formation, often hailed as a classic and straightforward system, played a pivotal role in shaping the identity of English football. Chapter 6 takes us back to a time when this formation reigned supreme, culminating in England's historic World Cup victory.

The Emergence of the 4-4-2 Formation

The 4-4-2 formation, characterized by four defenders, four midfielders, and two strikers, provided a balanced and pragmatic approach to the game. While it may appear conventional, its simplicity and versatility made it highly effective.

In this formation, the midfield was typically split into two central midfielders and two wide midfielders, creating a solid core while allowing for width in attack. The two strikers operated as a pair, often with one serving as the target man and the other as the poacher.

The Triumph of England in 1966

The golden moment for the 4-4-2 formation came in 1966 when England hosted and won the FIFA World Cup. Managed by Sir Alf Ramsey, the England team used the 4-4-2 system as the backbone of their success.

Key figures like Bobby Charlton and Geoff Hurst provided the attacking impetus, while Nobby Stiles and Martin Peters offered midfield stability. The partnership of Hurst and Roger Hunt up front showcased the potency of the two-striker system, with Hurst famously scoring a hat-trick in the World Cup final against West Germany.

Versatility and Adaptability

One of the strengths of the 4-4-2 formation was its adaptability. It could be used to play defensively or offensively, depending on the situation. When required, one of the midfielders could drop deeper to create a midfield diamond, adding an extra layer of support.

The formation also allowed for efficient transitions from defense to attack, as the wide midfielders could quickly join the attack when the team regained possession. This ability to switch between defensive solidity and offensive dynamism made the 4-4-2 a popular choice for many teams.

The Global Impact
The success of the 4-4-2 formation with England resonated globally. Many teams adopted this system, appreciating its balance and adaptability. In the following decades, several English clubs enjoyed domestic and international success employing the solid 4-4-2 formation.

The Evolution of Formations
While the 4-4-2 formation played a significant role in football history, it eventually gave way to more complex tactical systems. Modern football demands greater fluidity, flexibility, and specialization. However, the enduring legacy of the 4-4-2 can still be seen in various hybrid formations and strategies employed by teams today.

Chapter 7: Tiki-Taka: Spain's Artistic Mastery

Under the guidance of visionary coaches and skillful players, Spain introduced the footballing world to the captivating style of play known as Tiki-Taka. This mesmerizing system emphasized possession, precise passing, and artistic mastery of the beautiful game.

The Birth of Tiki-Taka

Tiki-Taka, a term that mimics the sound of quick, short passes, emerged as a tactical approach in the early 21st century. It was perfected by coaches like Pep Guardiola at Barcelona and Vicente del Bosque with the Spanish national team.

At its core, Tiki-Taka prioritized ball retention, quick circulation of possession, and intricate passing triangles. It was a system that relied heavily on teamwork, creativity, and technical excellence.

The Principles of Tiki-Taka

Tiki-Taka was characterized by several key principles:

- High-Intensity Pressing: When out of possession, teams employing Tiki-Taka applied high-pressure to win the ball back quickly. This approach prevented opponents from establishing their rhythm.

- Short Passing: Players focused on short, precise passes, maintaining a close connection and fluidity in their movements. This allowed for intricate ball circulation and the creation of passing triangles to break down defensive lines.

- Positional Play: Tiki-Taka teams emphasized positional awareness, with players constantly adjusting their positions to provide passing options. The movements were choreographed, creating a harmonious dance on the field.

- Patient Build-up: Tiki-Taka teams exhibited patience in their build-up play, often passing the ball laterally and backward to manipulate the opponent's defensive shape, waiting for the right moment to penetrate.

Success of Spain and Barcelona

The crowning achievement of Tiki-Taka was Spain's international success. Under Vicente del Bosque, Spain won the 2010 FIFA World Cup and the UEFA European Championship in 2008 and 2012. The Spanish national team showcased the power of possession football, dazzling fans and pundits alike with their intricate passing and fluid movements.

At the club level, Pep Guardiola's Barcelona became synonymous with Tiki-Taka. With players like Xavi Hernandez, Andres Iniesta, and Lionel Messi, the team dominated domestic and international competitions, including the UEFA Champions League.

Legacy of Tiki-Taka

Tiki-Taka's influence extended beyond Spain and Barcelona. Many top clubs and national teams sought to replicate its success by emphasizing possession and intricate passing in their strategies. However, the style also faced criticism for being overly cautious and possession-focused at times.

In the chapters ahead, we will continue our exploration of football formation evolution. We will delve into the resurgence of the 4-3-3 formation, the influence of the "False 9" phenomenon, and the impact of tactical hybrids. Join us in Chapter 8 as we uncover "The Rise of the 4-3-3: Modern Versatility," and explore how this formation added a new dimension to the beautiful game.

Chapter 8: The Rise of the 4-3-3: Modern Versatility

The 4-3-3 formation, with its adaptability and versatility, has become a staple in modern football. Chapter 8 delves into how this formation evolved to meet the ever-changing demands of the game, providing teams with a platform for both defensive solidity and attacking flair.

The Evolution of the 4-3-3

The 4-3-3 formation, characterized by four defenders, three midfielders, and three forwards, has a long history in football. However, it evolved significantly to meet the tactical demands of the modern era.

Initially, the 4-3-3 was often associated with a rigid structure, where the three forwards had distinct roles: a center forward flanked by two wingers. This formation was effective in providing width in attack but could be vulnerable defensively if the midfield lacked cover.

Total Football and the Dutch Influence

The adaptability and versatility of the 4-3-3 formation were elevated during the Total Football era, spearheaded by the Netherlands in the 1970s. Under coaches like Rinus Michels and players like Johan Cruyff, the 4-3-3 formation became a fluid system where players interchanged positions seamlessly.

The midfield trio was crucial in this evolution. A deep-lying playmaker, often known as the "number 6," orchestrated play from deep, while the two midfielders had the freedom to advance and support the attack. This allowed for dynamic movement and creativity on the field.

The Modern 4-3-3

In the modern game, the 4-3-3 formation has been adapted and fine-tuned to suit the strengths of individual teams and players. It remains one of the most versatile formations, capable of being both defensively solid and explosively attacking.

The wide forwards in a modern 4-3-3 often play a crucial role in providing goal-scoring opportunities. They can cut inside to shoot or create chances for others while full-backs provide width, contributing to the team's attacking options

Versatility and Tactical Hybrids

The 4-3-3 formation's versatility allows for tactical hybrids. Teams can shift seamlessly between a defensive structure, a possession-based game, and high pressing depending on the match situation. Coaches have experimented with variations such as the 4-2-3-1 and the 4-1-4-1, all built on the foundation of the 4-3-3.

Continued Influence

As we move forward in this exploration of football formations, we will examine the impact of the "False 9" phenomenon, the rise of the sweeper-keeper era, and the pressing game in detail. Join us in Chapter 9 as we uncover "The False 9 Phenomenon: Messi and Barcelona" and explore how this innovative role revolutionized the forward position, challenging conventional notions of striker play.

Chapter 9: The False 9 Phenomenon: Messi and Barcelona

In the world of football tactics and formations, the emergence of the False 9 role marked a revolutionary shift in the perception of the forward position. Chapter 9 delves into how this innovative role, personified by the brilliant Lionel Messi at Barcelona, transformed the game and challenged traditional notions of striker play.

The Birth of the False 9

The term "False 9" refers to a forward who operates in a deep-lying playmaker role, dropping into midfield areas to link up play, create goal-scoring opportunities, and unsettle the opposing defense. While the concept of a forward dropping deep was not entirely new, it was Messi's adaptation of the role that brought it to the forefront of tactical discussions.

Messi and Barcelona's Tiki-Taka

Lionel Messi's impact on the False 9 role cannot be overstated. Under the guidance of Pep Guardiola, Barcelona adopted a style of play known as Tiki-Taka, which relied heavily on ball retention, quick passing, and positional play. Messi, as the False 9, became the linchpin of this system.

By dropping deep and attracting defenders out of position, Messi created space for his teammates to exploit. His close ball control, dribbling ability, and vision allowed him to thread passes, make incisive runs, and score goals with remarkable consistency.

Challenging Defensive Lines

The False 9 role presented a unique challenge to opposing defenses. Traditional center-backs were accustomed to marking a central striker, but Messi's movements disrupted their positioning. If a defender followed Messi deep into midfield, it created gaps in the defensive line that other Barcelona players could exploit.

This dilemma forced defenders to make difficult decisions: stick with Messi and leave space elsewhere or maintain defensive shape and risk Messi's influence in deeper areas. It was a tactical conundrum that few teams could solve effectively.

Global Influence

Messi's success as a False 9 influenced tactical thinking worldwide. Coaches began to experiment with similar roles for their forwards, encouraging them to drop deep and contribute to build-up play. The False 9 concept transcended Barcelona and found its way into various leagues and national teams.

Evolution of Forward Play

The emergence of the False 9 challenged traditional notions of forward play, which had often been associated with scoring goals and playing closer to the opponent's penalty area. It highlighted the importance of a forward's all-around abilities, including playmaking, dribbling, and positional intelligence.

Chapter 10: The Sweeper-Keeper Era: Neuer and Bayern Munich

In **the ever-evolving** landscape of football tactics, the role of the goalkeeper has undergone a profound transformation. Chapter 10 takes us into the era of the "sweeper-keeper," exemplified by Manuel Neuer at Bayern Munich, and how goalkeepers have become pivotal in shaping the modern game.

The Traditional Goalkeeper Role

Historically, goalkeepers were primarily shot-stoppers and custodians of the penalty area. Their primary responsibility was to prevent the opposing team from scoring goals. They were not expected to be involved in outfield play or act as an additional outfield player.

Manuel Neuer and the Sweeper-Keeper Revolution

The rise of the sweeper-keeper can be largely attributed to Manuel Neuer, the world-class German goalkeeper. Neuer's style of play was characterized by his willingness to venture outside the penalty area to engage in outfield situations.

Neuer's attributes included exceptional reflexes, commanding presence in the box, and the ability to accurately distribute the ball with his feet.

The Sweeper-Keeper Role

The sweeper-keeper role involves several key responsibilities:

- High Defensive Line: Sweeper-keepers often play behind a high defensive line, reducing the space for opposing attackers and minimizing the risk of long balls over the top.
- Ball Distribution: Sweeper-keepers are expected to initiate attacks by distributing the ball accurately to outfield players. This includes both short passes to maintain possession and long, accurate passes to launch counterattacks.
- Sweeping: As the name suggests, they are also responsible for sweeping up loose balls or clearing danger outside the penalty area. This added dimension helps prevent potential goal-scoring opportunities for the opposition.

Impact on Tactics

The emergence of sweeper-keepers has had a profound impact on football tactics. It has allowed teams to adopt higher defensive lines, press higher up the pitch, and engage in a more possession-based style of play.

Sweeper-keepers have become a crucial part of the build-up phase, acting as an extra outfield player to progress the ball through the thirds of the pitch. This has led to a shift in how teams defend and attack.

Global Adoption

Manuel Neuer's success at Bayern Munich and with the German national team popularized the sweeper-keeper role. Many top clubs and national teams have since incorporated this style of play, with goalkeepers increasingly expected to possess both traditional shot-stopping skills and the ability to contribute to outfield play.

The Evolution Continues

As we continue our exploration of football formation evolution, we will delve into the high pressing game, the resurgence of three at the back, and the tactical innovations that define the modern era. Join us in Chapter 11 as we uncover "The High Pressing Revolution: Klopp's Liverpool" and explore how intense pressing has become a hallmark of successful teams in contemporary football.

Chapter 11: The High Pressing Revolution: Klopp's Liverpool

The concept of high pressing in football has evolved into a defining tactical strategy in the modern era. Chapter 11 delves into how Jürgen Klopp's Liverpool revolutionized the art of pressing, creating a high-energy style of play that has left a profound impact on the game.

The Birth of High Pressing

Pressing, or "gegenpressing" as it is often called in German, involves a team aggressively regaining possession of the ball in the opponent's half, usually within seconds of losing it. The idea is to exert intense pressure on the opponent, forcing turnovers and preventing them from settling into their attacking rhythm.

While pressing has been a part of football for decades, it was Jürgen Klopp's work at Borussia Dortmund and later Liverpool that brought high pressing to the forefront of tactical discussions

Klopp's Philosophy

Klopp's approach to pressing is characterized by several key principles:

- Collective Effort: High pressing relies on the entire team working collectively to win the ball back. It starts from the forwards and extends to midfielders and defenders, with everyone contributing to the press.
- Intense Pressure: Players are instructed to close down opponents quickly and apply pressure immediately after losing possession. The goal is to disrupt the opposition's passing lanes and create turnovers.
- Transition Play: Once possession is regained, teams that employ high pressing look to transition into attack rapidly. The opponent is often caught out of position, allowing for goal-scoring opportunities.
- Mental Toughness: High pressing demands physical fitness and mental toughness, as players must maintain a high work rate and focus for the duration of the match.

Liverpool's Success

Under Klopp's leadership, Liverpool's high pressing game became legendary. The team's relentless intensity, quick transitions, and ability to win the ball back in advanced areas made them one of the most formidable sides in Europe.

Liverpool won the UEFA Champions League in 2019 and the Premier League in 2020, with their high pressing style serving as a cornerstone of their success. Players like Mohamed Salah, Sadio Mané, and Roberto Firmino played key roles in executing Klopp's pressing philosophy.

Impact on the Game

Klopp's Liverpool not only achieved success but also influenced the broader footballing landscape. Teams around the world began to adopt high pressing as a tactical strategy, realizing its effectiveness in disrupting opponents and creating goal-scoring opportunities.

Continued Evolution

As football tactics continue to evolve, high pressing remains an integral part of many teams' strategies. However, coaches are constantly innovating and adapting their approaches to counter the press, making the tactical battles on the field even more intriguing.

In the chapters to come, we will explore the resurgence of three at the back, the role of wingbacks, and the tactical intricacies of possession football. Join us in Chapter 12 as we uncover "Three at the Back: The Defensive Renaissance" and explore how this formation has made a comeback in contemporary football, offering both defensive solidity and attacking versatility.

Chapter 12: Three at the Back: The Defensive Renaissance

The resurgence of the three at the back formation represents a defensive renaissance in modern football. Chapter 12 delves into how this tactical setup has evolved and why it has become a go-to choice for many teams seeking a balance between defensive solidity and attacking versatility.

The Evolution of Three at the Back

Three at the back, also known as a 3-4-3 or 3-5-2 formation, has a rich history in football. It was often seen as a defensive system, with three center-backs providing a solid foundation. However, in the modern era, it has evolved to incorporate attacking elements while maintaining defensive stability.

Versatility and Adaptability

One of the key features of three at the back formations is their adaptability. Teams can shift between defensive and attacking shapes seamlessly during matches. This flexibility allows for a more dynamic approach, with the formation accommodating various in-game situations.

Defensive Solidity

With three center-backs, teams in a three-at-the-back formation often have a numerical advantage in defense. This can help in dealing with opposition forwards and central attacking threats more effectively. The additional center-back can also contribute to ball recovery and distribution from deep.

Attacking Width

One of the reasons for the resurgence of three at the back formations is their ability to provide width in attack. Wingbacks, who play wide in the formation, can push forward to provide crosses and width while still maintaining a solid defensive shape when needed. This allows for greater attacking variety.

The Role of Wingbacks

Wingbacks are critical to the success of a three-at-the-back system. They are expected to cover vast areas of the pitch, contributing both defensively and offensively. Their ability to overlap and deliver accurate crosses adds a potent dimension to the team's attacking play.

Continued Evolution

The popularity of three at the back formations showcases football's ongoing evolution. Teams are constantly seeking ways to strike a balance between defense and attack, and the adaptability of this formation has made it a valuable tool in achieving that equilibrium.

As we move forward in our exploration of football formation evolution, we will unravel the intricacies of possession football, the influence of tactical hybrids, and the impact of modern football innovations. Join us in Chapter 13 as we delve into "Possession Football: Guardiola's Artistry" and explore how the meticulous art of maintaining possession has become a hallmark of tactical brilliance in the contemporary game.

Chapter 13: Inverted Wingbacks: Redefining Flank Play

In recent years, a fascinating evolution in football formations has emerged, altering the traditional roles of full-backs. Chapter 13 delves into the intriguing concept of inverted wingbacks, a tactical innovation that has redefined flank play and added a new dimension to modern football formations.

The Traditional Full-Back Role

Traditionally, full-backs were expected to hug the touchline, provide width, and deliver crosses into the box. Their primary roles were defensive, focused on marking wingers and preventing opposition attacks from wide areas. However, as football has evolved, so too have the responsibilities of full-backs.

Enter the Inverted Wingbacks

Inverted wingbacks or full-backs, are a tactical variation where full-backs play on the opposite side of their dominant foot, cutting inside rather than staying wide. This movement creates an overload in central midfield, providing numerical superiority and allowing for intricate passing combinations in the middle of the park.

Key Characteristics of Inverted Wingbacks

- Cutting Inside: Inverted wingbacks cut inside towards the center of the pitch, drawing opposition players out of position and creating space for midfielders and attackers.
- Playmaking Abilities: These players are often technically adept, possessing excellent passing, dribbling, and vision. Their ability to pick out teammates and initiate attacks from central areas adds a new creative dimension to the team's play.
- Defensive Awareness: While their primary focus is on attacking, inverted wingbacks must also be defensively aware. They need to track back and support the center-backs when the opposition launches attacks down the flanks.
- Goalscoring Threat: Inverted wingbacks, when cutting inside, often find themselves in goal-scoring positions. Their ability to shoot from distance or make late runs into the box can catch defenses off guard.

Tactical Implications

The introduction of inverted wingbacks has several tactical implications:

- Central Overload: Inverted wingbacks contribute to a numerical overload in central midfield, enabling the team to dominate possession and control the tempo of the game.
- Fluid Formations: Teams employing inverted wingbacks often exhibit fluid formations, seamlessly transitioning between different shapes depending on whether they are attacking or defending.
- Exploiting Space: By cutting inside, inverted wingbacks exploit the spaces between opposition defenders and midfielders. This movement can pull defenders out of position, creating gaps for other attacking players to exploit.
- Versatility: Inverted wingbacks add versatility to a team's attacking patterns. They can combine with central midfielders, play quick one-twos, and create goal-scoring opportunities in congested areas.

Conclusion: The Future of Full-Back Play

The rise of inverted wingbacks represents a shift in the tactical paradigm of full-back play. As teams continue to experiment with different formations and player roles, the versatility and creativity of inverted wingbacks offer an exciting glimpse into the future of football formations. Their ability to blend defensive solidity with attacking ingenuity makes them a potent weapon in the modern manager's tactical arsenal, challenging traditional notions and opening new avenues for strategic innovation in the beautiful game.

Conclusion: Embracing the Evolution of Football Formations

In the rich tapestry of football's history, formations have woven a narrative of innovation, adaptation, and creativity. From the pioneering days of rigid structures to the dynamic, fluid systems of today, the evolution of football formations stands as a testament to the sport's continual transformation.

Our journey through these chapters has been a voyage through time, exploring the tactical minds that have shaped the beautiful game. We've witnessed the meticulous artistry of possession football, the relentless pressing of modern high-press systems, and the fusion of styles in tactical hybrids.

Throughout this exploration, one truth remains evident: football is more than a game; it's a canvas for innovation and creativity. Coaches, players, and tacticians, past and present, have sculpted formations to fit their vision, pushing boundaries and challenging conventions. Each new chapter in football's evolution brings fresh excitement, promising unexpected strategies and inspiring the next generation of football enthusiasts.

In the rich tapestry of football's history, formations have woven a narrative of innovation, adaptation, and creativity. From the pioneering days of rigid structures to the dynamic, fluid systems of today, the evolution of football formations stands as a testament to the sport's continual transformation.

Our journey through these chapters has been a voyage through time, exploring the tactical minds that have shaped the beautiful game. We've witnessed the meticulous artistry of possession football, the relentless pressing of modern high-press systems, and the fusion of styles in tactical hybrids.

Throughout this exploration, one truth remains evident: football is more than a game; it's a canvas for innovation and creativity. Coaches, players, and tacticians, past and present, have sculpted formations to fit their vision, pushing boundaries and challenging conventions. Each new chapter in football's evolution brings fresh excitement, promising unexpected strategies and inspiring the next generation of football enthusiasts.

As fans, we find ourselves at the intersection of tradition and innovation, witnessing a sport that honors its roots while embracing the limitless possibilities of the future. The evolution of football formations is a reflection of our ever-changing world, where adaptability and inventive thinking reign supreme.

So, as we cheer for our favorite teams, let us celebrate not just the goals and victories but also the tactical brilliance and strategic nuances that shape every match. Let us anticipate the surprises yet to come, the unexplored formations waiting to be unveiled, and the tactical masterstrokes that will leave us in awe.